WHO WAS...

Florence
NIGHTINGALE

The Lady With the Lamp

CHARLOTTE MOORE

✳ SHORT BOOKS

First published in 2004 by

Short Books

15 Highbury Terrace

London N5 1UP

10 9 8 7 6 5 4 3 2

A CIP catalogue record for this book
is available from the British Library.

ISBN 1-904095-83-6

Printed in Great Britain by
Bookmarque, Croydon, Surrey.

For my goddaughter Sophia Clarke

Prologue

"I can never forget."

August, 1856. Lea Hurst, Derbyshire, England. The late afternoon light caught the mullioned windows of the great house so that it looked as if it were on fire. Lea Hurst stood high and proud above its terraced gardens that led down to rolling parkland. The magnificent trees – oaks, beeches and horse-chestnuts – stirred their summer leaves in the tiniest shiver of a breeze. The heavy air smelled of thunder.

William, Fanny, and Parthenope Nightingale waited in the drawing-room – waited for a fourth to complete their family circle. The dull tick of the clock on the mantelshelf, the whisper of the curtains at the window that opened on to the terrace – would the time never pass? William, father of the family, always

7

known as Wen, rose and paced the room, like a stork with his hooked nose and long, thin, stilt-like legs. Fanny, his wife, impatient and snappish, rebuked him.

'Wen! Keep still! You're making me nervous.'

Wen came to a halt at the bureau, where lay the closely-written sheets of the last letter from his missing daughter Florence. He fingered them absently; the pages rustled like dry leaves.

'This waiting is a torment,' sighed Parthenope for the hundredth time, laying her sleek head on her mother's shoulder.

'It is tedious for all of us, Parthe,' said her father, 'But Flo seems determined to keep us all guessing.'

'Flo was always the difficult one,' Fanny murmured. 'Aunt Mai says that she was determined to travel home alone. Oh, I could weep when I think of the plans that were laid for her! The Government offered a man-of-war to take her home in state, but no, Florence has to do things her way.'

'And the military bands!' mourned Parthe. 'Whole regiments would have marched out to meet her – their bands would have played her home! I can't help feeling disappointed in her.'

'Your disappointment, dear Parthe, is nothing

compared to that of the villagers,' put in Fanny. 'They had set their hearts on a triumphal arch; they wanted to draw her carriage themselves, right up to our very door.'

'If I were Flo, I would have gloried in it,' cried Parthe. She rose, moved to the circular rosewood table and fiddled with the cascade of hothouse flowers that stood at its centre, tweaking the lilies and tuberoses that poured out their sweet scent.

'Oh Parthe dear, pray don't tire yourself. I can't have you getting one of your heads. Bessy can deal with the flowers. Wen, dear, please ring for Bessy.'

'The flowers do not seem to me to need attention,' said Wen, 'but I will ring for Bessy if you wish.' He cleared his throat. 'When dear Flo does choose to return, I think it would be as well to refrain from calling her attention to the hurt feelings of the parishioners, or to any sensation of disappointment that may afflict us. Florence will be, I imagine, utterly exhausted. And besides, we should pay heed to Aunt Mai's words.'

'Which words in particular, Wen?'

Wen paused. 'Aunt Mai thinks that Florence is afraid of her fame.'

'Papa, that's nonsense. When has Flo ever been afraid of anything?'

***

Mrs Watson, the housekeeper at Lea Hurst, settled herself at her favourite window seat. She crossed her swollen ankles on an embroidered footstool and sipped her well-earned tea. A housekeeper's work was never done, but at this time of the evening she made a habit of taking half an hour off. The last few days had been a trial, with Mrs Nightingale issuing so many conflicting orders. 'The house must be cleaned from top to bottom; Miss Florence is expected any minute!' – but then: 'Why are you wasting time polishing windows when there is the linen to sort – no, we've heard nothing, it might be weeks until she returns.' Mrs Nightingale, always a temperamental employer, was like a cat on hot bricks.

To speak plainly, things had been tricky since the end of the war against Russia. A treaty had been signed for peace in the Crimea more than four months ago. Everyone had expected Miss Florence then, but no, she'd stayed on until the very last soldier had left her hospital at Scutari. Mrs Watson bit into her bread and butter, and smiled. That was Miss Florence all over. She never did things by halves. Mrs Watson had a soft spot for Miss Florence – always had done, ever since she was a child; long, long before she became a heroine, the darling of the British public. Why, there were even songs being written about her! There was a waxwork model of her, on show at Madame Tussauds, up in London somewhere! And how Mr Nightingale had chuckled over a Staffordshire figurine of his famous daughter! 'I can't say I would have recognised her, Mrs Watson,' he'd said, shaking his head over the pretty little china lady.

And now here they were, all waiting, and no word from Miss Florence. The not knowing was cruel. Mr and Mrs Nightingale weren't young anymore, and it was taking it out of them, this waiting. Still, that was Miss Florence's way. There was a hardness to her. It didn't surprise Mrs Watson that she'd said No to the battleship and the brass bands. Showing off wasn't Miss Florence's style. But how would she come? There'd be a telegram, surely, and a coach sent to meet her from London. She'd already sent a coach-load of things on ahead of her to Embley, the family's other home – her 'luggage' included a Russian orphan, a one-legged sailor boy, and a large Crimean puppy. That was typical of Miss Florence, too.

The sky to the west glowed apricot, but dark clouds were massing. A few fat drops of rain splashed on the stone terrace below Mrs. Watson's window. There wasn't much light left – but what was that, moving amongst the trees in the park? A slight female figure, dressed all in black, was walking towards the house, and pausing, every few steps, to touch the trunks of the trees as if they were old friends. Mrs Watson looked, and looked again. Could it be? – It was! She shrieked, burst into tears, and ran out to meet the most famous woman in Europe, the heroine of the Crimea, but to Mrs Watson, just her own Miss Florence.

***

The long, long day was done. She had been in Paris only the night before; she had boarded the first boat to Dover and caught the train to London. At eight in the morning she'd rung the bell at the Convent of the Bermondsey nuns – some of them had been her best nurses. She spent the morning praying with their Reverend Mother – giving thanks to God for the end of the war and the safe return of the nuns, but praying even more fervently for the thousands of soldiers who would never return; who lay, victims of starvation and disease as well as wounds, in the burial grounds of the Crimea. And she made a solemn vow, that she would never rest until she had avenged their cruel and unnecessary deaths.

That afternoon, still alone, she took a train north, to Derbyshire. She had draped a shawl over her head and walked unrecognised from the station to Lea Hurst; up the long drive, through the rich parkland, beautiful in its summer dress. Home she had walked to Wen, Fanny and Parthe – her beloved, infuriating, unchanging family!

And now the tears, the embraces, the torrents of talk were over. Florence was alone in her room. She was tired to the bone, but she could not sleep. Sometimes she felt as if she would never sleep again. She had seen Hell, and she was set apart. As she watched the moon climb free of the snatching clouds, she scribbled the same phrase over and over – 'I can never forget.' In the weeks to come, she would find her

pen shaping the words in letters, on the margins of
books, on any scrap of paper – 'I can never forget.'
Her life's work lay ahead of her.

Chapter One

The Call

She was named after the place where she was born – Florence, the gayest city in Europe.

Her parents were enjoying an extended honeymoon. They had married two years earlier, in 1818, and had been touring Europe ever since. The Napoleonic Wars had come to an end; British people could travel freely again, and Fanny and William Nightingale made the most of it. They both came from well-to-do families. Wen – his nickname came from his initials – had no need to work for a living. And, as Fanny said of her own family, 'We Smiths never thought of anything all day long but our own ease and pleasure.' All they had to do was enjoy themselves.

This suited Fanny perfectly. She was beautiful, lively, and generous to the point of extravagance. At every city on their European tour, Fanny sought out the most interesting and important people and made friends with them. Her life was a whirlwind of dinner parties, balls, trips to the opera and theatre.

Wen was a different creature altogether. He smiled and went along with Fanny's plans, but without her he would have skipped the parties. In his Cambridge days he had been well known for his wit and intelligence, but also for his indolence. He loved books and intellectual conversation, but he let his talents go to waste. 'My father,' said Florence, years later, 'is a man who has never known what struggle is.'

Wen had a handsome aquiline nose and an impressive brow. He had a habit of propping his tall, thin body against doors and mantelpieces. He even had a writing desk especially made so that he could stand instead of sitting. Fanny loved comfort, fine clothes, the best food and wine. Wen was indifferent to such things. As long as he had quiet hours to read and study, he did not care whether he was in a palace or a pigsty. Wen and Fanny loved each other, but they were not a well-matched couple.

Their first daughter was born in Naples a year after their wedding. They gave her the Greek name for Naples: Parthenope. A year later, on 12th May 1820, the second baby was born. She was christened Florence in the drawing-room of the grandly furnished villa where the family was staying. How could the Nightingales have guessed that, fifty years on, many thousands of baby girls all over the world would be named Florence in honour of this baby? Poor Parthenope. Her name never caught on.

When little Florence was just taking her first toddling steps, the family returned to England. Wen designed a house for them – Lea Hurst, a fantastical Gothic creation which seemed to float above the rolling Derbyshire countryside. Wen was proud of himself, but Fanny found fault.

'My dearest, it is too cold! Winters will be quite impossible. And so far from all our London friends! And it is much too small to entertain people properly – why, there are only fifteen bedrooms!'

So Wen bought a second house, Embley Park, near the New Forest. Embley was warm, the gardens were glorious, the shooting was good, and lots of cousins lived nearby.

Throughout Florence's childhood the pattern never varied. Summers at Lea Hurst, the rest of the year at Embley, with visits to London in spring and autumn.

The sisters – nicknamed Flo and Pop – should have had an idyllic childhood. There were ponies, dogs, cats, and birds, acres of space and plenty of playmates – there were twenty-seven first cousins, for a start. Every Christmas there was a ball just for the children. They acted plays and built tree houses. They were taken to the Isle of Wight for swimming and sailing. And they had the companionship of their father, whom they adored, and who was full of jokes and games.

And yet Flo was not a happy child. Fanny could not understand her strange, moody, obstinate daughter. Flo was prettier than Pop. She was slim and graceful, with thick glossy chestnut hair and a lovely complexion. She was cleverer than Pop, too. Although she was younger, Flo was the dominant one. She had a passion for neatness and order; Pop's scatterbrain ways drove her mad.

'Dear Pop,' she wrote, aged ten, 'I have not put your scrapbook anywhere, but one day I saw it in the drawer of the music room next to the bow window and I think it very odd you did not think of looking for it there!!!'

Flo was admired by everyone, but she shrugged off the praise. She had a secret. She was a monster. She knew this from her earliest years. She was not like other people – she was like a visitor from another world. One day she would be found out, and this was her private terror.

By the age of six, Flo knew that she despised the rich, easy life her parents led. She longed to do something useful, something noble. When Pop pulled her dolls to bits, Flo stitched them back together, and nursed them tenderly. When her dog injured his paw, she bound it in splints as carefully as any doctor. When she found a dead blue-tit, she gave it a state funeral and wrote an epitaph –

'Tomtitty bird! Why art thou dead
Thou who dost bear upon thy head
A crown! But now thou art on thy death-bed,
My Tom Tit.'

She escaped into a dream world, and told herself endless stories in which she was the heroine.

Flo was too clever. That was Fanny's opinion.

Visitors gasped at her amazing intelligence. Fanny wished they wouldn't. What use was cleverness to a girl? A good marriage, raising children, entertaining friends, organising servants – that was the destiny of girls like Parthenope and Florence Nightingale. Women in those days didn't have careers. It just didn't happen. Too much cleverness only made you restless.

Wen disagreed. The girls never went to school – upper-class girls didn't. They were taught at home by governesses. But when Florence was twelve, Wen decided that his daughters were too bright for any governess. He decided to teach them himself. Tutors came in for music and drawing, but Wen taught them Greek, Latin, German, French, Italian, history and philosophy. At Flo's earnest request he added mathematics.

He had high standards, and he made them work long hours. Pop was bored and rebellious. It wasn't long before Wen gave up on her, and the family divided – Flo and Wen together in the library, poring over Greek verbs, Pop and Fanny in the drawing-room, arranging flowers, receiving visitors, and writing letters to all those cousins.

In 1834, Wen stood for parliament as a Liberal candidate. He lost the election, because he wouldn't bribe people to vote for him. Fanny, disappointed, turned her ambitions on her daughters. If she couldn't have an M.P. for a husband, then she could at least make sure her daughters married rich and powerful men.

It was Fanny's duty, as a mother, to make sure her daughters 'came out' well. No, more than duty – it was one of the high points of a mother's life. Upper-class girls 'came out' in their late teens. 'Coming out' meant making the transition from the schoolroom to the ballroom, from childhood to the adult world. They put their hair up, and decked themselves in a whole new wardrobe of grown-up clothes. For the best part of a year, they were paraded by their mothers at an endless range of social events, where they met suitable young men. In those few months, their fate would be decided, for better or for worse.

Fanny could hardly wait. Her girls were so close in age, they could 'come out' together. She was going to do this in style – the world would sit up and take notice.

But first the house had to be brought up to scratch.

Embley seemed cramped and old-fashioned. It must be enlarged and improved. While the work was in progress, the Nightingales would take the girls on a tour of Europe.

They would revisit the places where they had been so happy on their honeymoon. The girls – Florence and Parthe, no longer Flo and Pop – would meet interesting people, improve their languages, see the world. And then they would come back and be snapped up by the most eligible bachelors in England.

Wen designed an enormous carriage for their tour of Europe – family inside, servants on the roof. It was equipped with devices for reading, writing, eating and resting in comfort. It would be pulled by six horses. Wen was enjoying himself. He loved travelling, and he loved making plans for the aggrandisement of Embley. The family buzzed with schemes and discussions.

And in the middle of it all, Florence received a call from God.

Chapter Two

The Wild Swan

She was not quite seventeen, and she spent more time in her dream world than out of it. But the voice that called her was not a dream voice. Like Joan of Arc, she heard a voice outside herself, speaking human words. God was calling her to his service. She never stopped believing that, for the rest of her long life.

What did God want her to do? Ah, that was not so clear. She didn't even think of nursing. In the 1830s, nurses were dirty, drunken creatures. They had no training, they were just hard-bitten women who put up with horrible hospital conditions in exchange for a little money, bread and beer, and the chance of canoodling with the male patients. No one could have dreamed that a well-born girl like Florence could become a nurse.

She knew she loved caring for people and animals. She was famous in the family for her way with babies, and she felt that God wanted her to use this side of her nature. All she had to do was wait, and He would show her exactly how. For the first time in years, she was full of confidence and peace.

The Nightingales set off for the Continent in their eccentric carriage. Florence loved it. At Chartres she sat up all night – she couldn't stop gazing at the moonlight on the cathedral. At Nice she discovered a passion for dancing. Genoa was 'like an Arabian Nights dream come true'. In Florence, her birthplace, she became, she told her cousin Hilary, 'music-mad'. In Paris, she made great and lasting friendships with intellectuals and politicians.

Fanny was delighted. Her strange, stubborn daughter had blossomed into a great social success. Back in London, in a few months' time the girls would be presented at court; they would make brilliant marriages. Fanny thought that nothing could stand in their way. But Florence's conscience was a stumbling block.

Florence was not short of admirers. One, in particular, was tempting. Richard Monckton Milnes was a poet, a well-travelled charmer who knew everyone. 'If Christ came back to earth,' quipped a friend, 'the first thing to happen would be that Monckton Milnes would invite him to breakfast.' But he had a serious side, too. He worked tirelessly for the rights of child criminals, who, he said, should not be put in adult prisons.

Monckton Milnes spent so much time with the Nightingales that he became like one of the family. He was desperately in love. Everyone urged Florence to marry him. But if she married, she reasoned, what would become of her own ambitions? With a husband, maybe children, how could she obey God's call?

She worked it all out in a private note. 'I have an intellectual nature which requires satisfaction, and that would find it in him. I have a passional nature which requires satisfaction, and that would find it in him. I have a moral, an active nature which requires satisfaction, and that would not find it in his life.'

The answer had to be 'no'. Monckton Milnes was bitterly disappointed, but hardly more so than Fanny Nightingale.

Florence turned her mind away from thoughts of romance, and spent more and more time working for people less fortunate than herself. She loved to visit the poor in their tumbledown cottages, to play with and teach the ragged children, to bring good food and medicine to the sick. Fanny disapproved, but Florence slipped out when nobody was looking. She nursed members of the family – her favourite little cousin, 'my boy Shore', had a bad attack of measles, but Florence saw him through. Her old nanny, Mrs Gale, fell ill. Florence spent all her time with her; Mrs Gale died holding her hand.

Slowly the truth dawned. She was to be a nurse! That was the service to which God had called her. Never mind the terrible reputation of nurses, never mind the disgusting condition of hospitals – she could change all that. She could achieve anything, if only her family would let her...

She paced the large airy rooms and long corridors of Embley. What a wonderful hospital it would make! Not like any hospital anyone had ever heard of. Not like the local infirmary at Salisbury, overrun with rats, sixty beds crammed into each ward, broken windows boarded up, walls streaming with moisture, the stench so bad it could make you physically sick. No, Florence had a vision in her mind of a clean, sunlit, quiet place, where patients came, not to die, but to recover. Was she mad?

She had to start somewhere. Salisbury Infirmary was better than nothing. Her heart pounding, she asked her parents' permission to work there as a volunteer. Parthe had hysterics. Fanny went white with rage. 'You want to have an affair with some low, vulgar surgeon,' she accused. Wen was disgusted. Had he educated his favourite daughter for this?

Florence was defeated, but she fought back. Secretly she studied health reports, rising before dawn so that she could work uninterrupted. She read about a well-run hospital with an orphanage attached. It was run by nuns, at Kaiserwerth in Germany. She would get there, by hook or by crook.

***

In 1847 her great friends Selina and Charles Bracebridge took her to Rome. She loved it. At a service in St Peter's, she spotted a beautiful dark-eyed girl of five. Her name was Felicetta, and she was a penniless orphan. Immediately, Florence had her placed in a convent school where she was well looked after. For many years, Florence sent money for 'my little Felicetta' out of her dress allowance.

Later, she travelled to Egypt and Greece. Wherever she went she collected animals. Two chameleons slept on her bed. She befriended tortoises, and a cicada called Plato. At the Parthenon she rescued a baby owl from some Greek boys. She named her Athena. Athena was a fierce little creature, but Florence tamed her by using the fashionable trick of mesmerism, a kind of hypnosis. After that, Athena went everywhere with her, peeping out of her pocket. Alas, Athena ate poor Plato.

But travelling was only a distraction from the problem. Her journey over, she was stuck at home again, wondering how she was to fulfil her ambition. At thirty years old, she still had not broken free from her family. Fanny's grand dreams for her daughters had come to nothing; Parthe had yet to find a husband. Parthe lived at home, often in a state bordering on hysteria. The emotional demands she put on her sister were enormous. Florence might have resisted marriage, but was still a slave to a pointless

28

domestic routine. 'Women don't consider themselves as human beings at all,' she fumed, 'There is no tyranny worse than the petty, grinding tyranny of an English family.'

She planned to escape to Kaiserwerth Hospital. But Parthe made herself ill with worry at the thought of dear Flo doing anything so horrid and dangerous. Parthe lived and breathed Flo; she seemed to have no life of her own. She wanted to devour Flo with her hysterical affection, and Flo didn't blame her. 'Parthe,' she said, 'is like a child playing in God's garden.'

But the playing got rough when Florence at last broke loose. She had agreed to spend six months as Parthe's devoted slave, obeying her every whim; this was supposed to be for the good of Parthe's mental and physical health. When the six months was up, Florence set off for Kaiserwerth, supported by her friends. Parthe reacted like a wounded animal. The nerves of the whole family, servants included, were stretched to breaking-point by the sound of her howling. Florence was firm in her resolve to stick to her plan, but she had to do something, make some gesture, to show her sister that she was not going just to spite her.

The night before her departure, Florence stood outside Parthe's door, listening. In her hand she held some bracelets, pretty trinkets that had been given to her by aunts and cousins to mark birthdays and other special occasions. Florence wasn't interested in jewellery. She knew they would mean far more to Parthe than they meant to her. She listened until the sobbing behind the door had quietened, then gently she knocked, and entered.

Parthe's appearance was shocking. Always slender, she had become emaciated; determined to show how passionately she objected to Florence's plan, she had all but stopped eating. Her once-glossy hair was lank and dishevelled, her eyes swollen and red with weeping. She stared at Florence, unsmiling, unspeaking.

'Parthe,' said Florence, 'Put out your hand.'

Parthe obeyed. Florence poured the bracelets into her palm, closed her fingers round them.

'I want you to have these jewels,' she continued, 'Because I want you to know that I do, sincerely, love you. I wish you nothing but good, dear Parthe. Please keep them, as a token of my feeling for you.' Her words sounded false and formal, but talking to Parthe in her crazed state didn't feel like talking to a human being.

Parthe held the bracelets up to the candle, to admire the way they glowed and glittered. An expression of pleasure softened her pale face.

'But Flo, they're yours! Here's the one Cousin Hilary gave you for your twenty-first birthday – it's so pretty! You must keep them.'

'Bracelets,' said Florence, 'have no place in a nurse's wardrobe.'

The pleasure was gone. Parthe's face became a distorted mask of hatred. 'How dare you speak that word aloud!' she spat. 'Don't come here to remind me of the dishonour you are bringing on our family!' And with a single movement, unexpectedly violent from one so frail, she flung the trinkets into her sister's face.

It was overwhelming – the pain of the hard-edged jewels slashing across her cheek, the horror of her sister's twisted features, the venom in her voice. Florence fainted, staggered, fell.

She revived to find Parthe bending over he, tears falling fast. 'Oh Flo, dearest Flo, forgive me! It's just that I can't bear to think of it...'

'Don't think of it, then,' said Florence, all her

determination restored. 'Close your mind, make believe that I am travelling for the good of my health. I go tomorrow, and neither you, nor anybody else, can prevent me.'

***

Florence got to Kaiserwerth, and put her family's agonies out of her mind. At last, she had broken free. She was in heaven. Everyone rose at five; the work was hard, but that suited her. She loved the order, the discipline, the sense of being useful as she nursed the sick and taught the children. Gone was the wasteful luxuriousness that so irritated her at home. The peasant diet of broth, bread and vegetables made her feel healthy. And there was fun to be had, too. The orphans' birthdays were celebrated with dressing-up, flowers, story-telling and singing.

Though Kaiserwerth wasn't perfect – 'the hygiene was horrible' Florence later wrote – she gained valuable medical experience. She took part in operations, even amputations. This was secret. It was considered indecent for any woman to witness an operation, let alone a gentlewoman like Florence.

But she was only a visitor. After a few months, she had to go home. Fanny and Parthe met her, but treated her as if she had just left prison. 'They would hardly speak to me,' wrote Florence.

Now Florence was even more desperate for a career. Parthe could rant and rave until she was blue in the face – Florence knew she had to follow the call from God, and Kaiserwerth had shown her the way. On 12th May 1850 she had written a note to herself: 'Today I am thirty – the age Christ began his Mission. Now no more childish things, no more vain things, no more love, no more marriage. Now, Lord, let me only think of Thy will.'

Then the perfect job appeared. The Institute for the Care of Sick Gentlewomen in Distressed Circumstances, in Harley Street, London, needed a superintendent. The 'sick gentlewomen' were mainly governesses who became destitute once they could no longer work. Harley Street was a respectable neighbourhood; the Institute was run by ladies. Fanny and Parthe disapproved, of course, but they had to admit that it was respectable. It was a far cry from the horrors of Salisbury Infirmary. If Flo was wrong-headed enough to insist on a job, then this job seemed less disgusting than most.

So Florence took over. Her organisational skills were phenomenal. She delighted in transforming the Institute into a thoroughly efficient, modern nursing home. 'I am living in an ideal world of lifts, gas, baths, and double and single wards,' she wrote to her cousin Hilary. The 'distressed gentlewomen' adored her. One climbed out of bed at night to get cold feet, just so Miss Nightingale would rub them warm again.

'She stands perfectly alone, half way between God and his creatures,' said the novelist Elizabeth Gaskell, who knew Florence at this time. Mrs Gaskell described Florence's 'perfect grace and lovely appearance' and said she had a good sense of humour and was an excellent mimic. And yet this graceful creature had the institute organised and running smoothly in six months.

London was a place to avoid in summer. There was no proper drainage, the drinking water was little better than sewage, and in hot weather diseases multiplied by the hour. Richer Londoners took off to their country retreats; the poor just sweated it out. In August 1854 cholera broke out in Soho; Florence went as a volunteer to the Middlesex Hospital to nurse the prostitutes who fell victim to the epidemic more quickly than any other social group. The filthy, drunken women were crazed with terror and pain, and Florence was 'up day and night, undressing them... poor creatures, staggering off their beat!'

'Oh Mrs Gaskell!' exclaimed Fanny, hearing an edited account of Florence's activities, 'We are ducks who have hatched a wild swan!'

How could Florence guess that the agonies of the prostitutes would be nothing compared to the suffering she would witness only three months later? For one of the greatest catastrophes of the nineteenth century was about to happen – the Crimean War.

Chapter Three

"Theirs But To Do Or Die"

The Crimean War has been called 'one of the bad jokes of history'. The power of Turkey was in decline; the French and English governments were alarmed by Russia's ambition to muscle in on Turkey's weakness.

In March 1853 Russia demanded that the Orthodox Church in Turkey should be placed under Russian control. Turkey refused. Russia hit back by occupying Turkey's Danubian principalities. The Turks could not ignore this insult; they declared war.

When a Turkish squadron was destroyed at Sinope on the Black Sea, Britain and France decided to come to Turkey's aid. The British had been at peace since the end of the Napoleonic Wars nearly forty years earlier. The army had grown rusty with disuse – the Crimean campaign was to prove just how disorganised it was.

Lord Raglan led the British troops. There were 26,000 men, and they looked smart in their red uniforms. Their brass bands and little drummer boys made a grand show, but many were raw recruits with very little training. There were no soldiers in reserve to back them up. Four of the five infantry division – the foot soldiers – were commanded by officers in their sixties and seventies who had fought in the Peninsula War, long ago. The cavalry, with their superb horsemanship, were the pride of the army. The Light Brigade was led by Lord Cardigan, the Heavy Brigade by Sir James Scarlett. But – as the famous Charge of the Light Brigade was to prove so horribly – horses were defenceless against the onslaught of Russian cannons.

The Crimea, the theatre of war, was in that part of the world now known as Ukraine. The British troops set sail from Portsmouth; their long voyage took them across the Mediterranean, through the Aegean Sea, into the Sea of Marmora and up the Bosphorus, the stretch of water that divides Europe from Asia. They disembarked at Varna, which is now in Bulgaria but was then in Turkey. Most of the soldiers had never left Britain before; they were exhausted and bewildered after weeks on the crowded ships. But the worst part of their journey was still to come. To reach the Crimea – Crim Tartary – the army had to cross the Black Sea.

The French army were better organised than their British allies. Together, the French and British managed to win the Battle of the River Alma, because their rifles proved more effective than the Russian muskets. But after the battle, the real horror began. There was no treatment for the wounded. They lay on straw mixed with manure in farmyards. Surgeons amputated limbs without anaesthetics, working by moonlight because there were no lamps. Cholera broke out.

The sick and wounded were carried back across the Black Sea to the Barrack Hospital at Scutari. The ships, designed for 250 people, had to take 1500. Men lay in heaps of excrement, too weak to move, rolling on top of one another as the ship lurched.

The arrival was hardly better. The Barrack Hospital was enormous, dirty and tumbledown, with no beds, blankets, food or clean water. Half-naked men lay in lines on the bare, unwashed floors. A handful of doctors could not hope to deal with the thousands of patients.

Soldiers had always suffered. The social hierarchy of the army was rigid. The officers, well-fed and well-educated, came from the upper classes. But the ordinary soldiers, the 'privates', were working-class men who were regarded by those in authority as little better than criminals. 'The scum of the earth enlisted for drink,' the Duke of Wellington had called them; no government had ever thought highly enough of privates to provide them with decent living conditions or good medical treatment. But in this war, the first proper war since the defeat of Napoleon in 1815, there was an important difference: the British public got to know how brutal the conditions were.

William Howard Russell, a reporter for the *Times*, sent back reports that were enough to make your hair stand on end. Russell was the first ever war correspondent. He was a fearless man with a passion for the truth. He got into the trenches, talked to the men on guard, investigated hospitals and the transport ships that carried the sick. The soldiers' sufferings made him furious, and in his dispatch in the *Times* he let his feelings show. 'Not only,' he wrote, 'are the men kept, in some cases for a week, without the hand of a medical man coming near their wounds; not only are they left to expire in agony, unheeded and shaken off, though catching desperately at the surgeon as he makes his rounds through the fetid ship, but now… the men must die through the medical staff of the British Army having forgotten that old rags are necessary for the dressing of wounds.'

The British public, reading his words, took action. 'The *Times* Fund' was started to supply the soldiers with comforts and necessities. Sidney Herbert, the Secretary at War, was responsible for the treatment of the sick and wounded. He was also a great friend of Florence Nightingale. On Sunday 15th October 1854, horrified by what he read in the *Times*, Sidney Herbert wrote to Florence, asking her to lead a party of nurses out to the Barrack Hospital. 'There is but one person in England that I know who would be capable of organising and superintending such a scheme,' he wrote.

And that one person was already busy preparing for the task. She had gathered a troop of thirty-eight nurses; at exactly the same time as Sidney Herbert was writing his letter, she was busy writing to him to ask permission to go to Scutari. It was an extraordinary coincidence. 'My own dearest noblest Flo,' wrote Liz Herbert, Sidney's wife, 'I knew you would do it.'

Only six days later, Florence and her nurses were ready to leave. In the hurry of packing, Athena was accidentally shut in the attic, where she died. When Florence held the little feathery corpse, she burst into tears. 'Poor little beastie, it was odd how much I loved you.'

She showed no other emotion on the eve of departure. But in her pocket-book she enclosed a letter from her former lover, Richard Monckton Milnes. 'So you are going to the East,' he wrote, 'you can undertake that, when you could not undertake me.'

Chapter Four

"Lo! In that hour of misery
A lady with a lamp I see ..."
Longfellow

It was a bedraggled huddle of nurses that disembarked at Scutari on a bleak November morning. The voyage had been stormy, the seasickness terrible. But now here they were at the Barrack Hospital. They had to pull themselves together; prove how tough they were.

They received a frosty welcome. The army doctors didn't want women around. They had never worked with female nurses before. Women got in the way. They couldn't cope with blood and guts, they would waste time fussing about the way they looked and what their living conditions were like. They would flirt with the men or, worse still, read them sermons. That was the opinion of Dr Menzies, the senior medical officer. He was confident that Miss Nightingale and her nurses would soon scuttle back to England in horror.

And it would not have been surprising if they had. The Barrack Hospital was a forbidding place. 'Abandon hope all ye that enter here' – that's what should have been written over its doorway, said Florence. It was a huge square building, a tower at each corner, one side gutted by fire. The courtyard was a sea of mud and rubbish. Turkish locals had set up tents all round it to sell bad alcohol to those soldiers well enough to buy it. It was more or less poison – some men ended up back in hospital after drinking it. Under the hospital, in the pitch-dark, stinking cellars, lived over 200 prostitutes, many with babies.

Florence and the nurses were given only six small rooms between them, and no food or furniture. In one room lay the corpse of a Russian general – nobody had bothered to move him. The nurses were experienced women who had seen a thing or two in their time, but this was a bit too much. They started to grumble. Florence was firm. 'We are here to work,' she reminded them. In England, she'd been told that no supplies were needed. Thank heavens she'd trusted her own instincts and bought food and equipment en route! She distributed some food amongst the nurses, since the army would not allow them rations.

Florence realised they would need patience. They would have to prove their usefulness, win the confidence of the doctors. 'Never enter the wards,' she ordered, 'unless invited to do so by a doctor.' Until then, they must occupy themselves with washing and mending, filling sacks with straw to make mattresses. The nurses were unhappy. They'd come all this way to nurse the poor suffering fellows, not to sew! But Florence knew what she was doing, and her air of authority carried weight.

Florence and her team had arrived ten days after the Battle of Balaclava, the day before the Battle of Inkerman. If conditions were already bad, they became ten times worse when the sick and wounded began to arrive after Inkerman. This battle was fiercely fought on a hilltop in swirling fog. Many suffered from frostbite and exposure as well as wounds. Earlier, in warmer weather, they had been ordered to throw away their backpacks because they were too heavy; now they had nothing extra to wear. Their rations were salt meat and dried peas, which had to be swallowed raw. A hurricane blew away the army tents, and sank several supply ships.

After Inkerman, there were 2,300 patients in the Barrack Hospital. Florence calculated that there were four miles of men lying along the corridors but only thirty a day could be cleaned, without the nurses' help. Nearly all of them had diarrhoea, but there were only twenty chamber pots in the entire building. These were tipped into two vast wooden tubs. Nobody took responsibility for emptying the tubs.

The men were covered in body lice, 'as thick as the letters on a page of print.' There was no privacy whatsoever. Amputations were carried out in full view of everyone. The death rate from the amputations was eighty-two per cent.

The doctors had never faced such a crisis before. Reluctantly, they turned to Miss Nightingale and her nurses. Would they please... er... help? The women cheered silently. At last they could stop mending sheets and get down to the proper business of nursing.

The workload was unbelievable. Florence was often on her feet for twenty-four hours without a break. A lot of the problems were caused by too much 'red tape'. None of the army staff would do anything unless they received an official order, on paper. For example, one day an enormous load of 27,000 shirts arrived, but the Purveyor would not release them for three weeks because he had not received an order. Meanwhile, the men lay shivering in blood-stained rags. Some supply ships crossed the Black Sea three times before official permission to unload them was granted.

But Florence had government backing. She had the support of Sidney Herbert, Secretary for War. This meant she could cut the 'red tape' and get things moving. She set up a 'Government Store House' so that when supplies arrived they could be unpacked quickly. She bought supplies in Constantinople – her first order was for 200 scrubbing brushes – and she hired Turkish workers to fetch and carry. She paid for this out of the *Times* fund, and out of her own pocket. She rented a house near the hospital, installed huge boilers, and turned it into a laundry. Some of the soldiers' wives had followed them to the war; now

Florence set them to work on the washing.

Feeding everybody was a nightmare. There was only one kitchen, and the only cooking apparatus was thirteen coppers – like gigantic boilers – each holding 450 pints. The meat ration was distributed to the orderlies in charge of each ward. All the meat was boiled together in the coppers, so each orderly had to mark out his ward's hunk of meat from the others, and they were inventive in how they did this. Red rags, rusty nails, buttons, surgical scissors, odd bits of uniform, were attached to the joints and flung into the cooking pot. Florence did not have our understanding of how infection spreads – germs had not been discovered in 1854 – but she did have a horror of dirt, and the marked-out meat disgusted her.

When the cook had had enough, the fires were extinguished, the joints fished out and given to the orderlies. If your joint had gone in last, it might be almost raw. Then the meat was divided by weight. If your portion was all bone and gristle, too bad. Florence suggested that the bones be removed before weighing, but was told, 'It would require a new regulation of service to bone the meat.'

There were few vegetables. Once a shipload of

cabbages was thrown into the harbour because it was not consigned to anyone. Florence set up new kitchens, and ordered food from local markets.

And then in March 1855 Alexis Soyer arrived. He worked at the Reform Club in London and was the celebrity chef of his day. In London, he'd heard about the soldiers' abominable diet, and he'd come to help, at his own expense. He was a flamboyant Frenchman who thoroughly understood food. And he got on famously with Miss Nightingale. Within days, he transformed the kitchens, and, using only the army rations, produced delicious, nourishing soups and stews. He invented ovens for bread and biscuits and a 'Scutari teapot' that would keep tea hot for fifty men at a time. When he walked through the wards carrying his soup tureen the men clapped and cheered.

Alexis Soyer was a great favourite, but there was one person the soldiers adored above all others, and that was Miss Nightingale herself. They treated her with the utmost respect.

'Before she came, there was cussin' and swearin',' recalled one soldier, 'But after that it was as 'oly as a church.' With the nurses, officers and orderlies, Florence could be stern, abrupt, unbending – 'I never gave or took an excuse.' But with the soldiers she was always tender and kind. She never let any man die alone. She nursed the worst cases herself. During that first winter she witnessed 2,000 deathbeds.

At night she patrolled the wards, carrying her lamp. The silence was broken only by the groans and sighs of suffering. Florence paused by the worst cases, checked that amputated stumps were protected by special pillows, held tin cups of water to parched lips, murmured reassurance to men whose sleep was made restless by feverish dreams. A hand reached out to touch the hem of her dress. Florence, stooping to listen, observed the receding gums and flaking skin of scurvy. 'Miss Nightingale,' whispered the soldier, 'It is a comfort to see you pass, even. I never thought you'd stop and speak to me.'

Florence reached into her pocket and brought out an orange. Vitamins had yet to be discovered, but she knew that citrus fruit was the best remedy against scurvy. 'Here,' she said, 'This will do you good. Let me peel it for you.'

'No, no, ma'am. There's nowt wrong with my hands. You see to the next fellow that needs you.'

Florence moved on. The soldier pushed the orange

out of sight, under his straw-stuffed pillow. He longed to taste its sour-sweet tang, but he had no intention of eating it. That orange was a sacred relic; Miss Nightingale's hands had touched it. The orange – black and shrivelled – still survives today, in the Nightingale family collection.

The light of the lamp moved through the dark, vaulted room, darting here and there like a firefly.

In the doorway, Dr John Hall, Chief of Medical Staff, looked on with folded arms. He was a recent arrival at Scutari; he'd got the job because of his reputation for toughness – some would call it cruelty. Some of the lesser doctors had come round to Miss Nightingale, and respected her stamina and skill. Not Dr John Hall. In his opinion, Miss Nightingale was nothing but a nuisance, daring to infiltrate male territory with her fancy ideas. Women were too soft for war; they caused nothing but trouble. This Miss Nightingale had suggested – tried to insist, even – that the surgeons used chloroform to mask the pain of amputations. True, there were unused supplies of chloroform in the store cupboards, but Dr Hall had no intention of using them. Chloroform was for weaklings. 'Miss Nightingale,' he had boomed, 'you will spoil the brutes.'

He'd been appalled by tales of the soldiers' adoration of this interfering do-gooder, and he'd come down into the wards at this ungodly hour to see for himself. The lamp came to rest in a corner where the stench, which hung everywhere like an evil fog, seemed particularly bad.

The nurses had told Florence earlier that day of a new arrival who refused to be nursed. He was ashamed of his filthy, naked state. 'My own mother would not touch me,' he said, 'How can I let a lady near me?' He pulled the tattered remnants of his blood-soaked greatcoat over his vermin-infested body and turned his face to the wall. Death was all he wished for.

Florence made a mental note to tackle this case herself. Now, she'd found him. She set her lamp on the floor near his feet, so that there was light enough to see what she was doing, but not so much that the man felt exposed. In her clear, low voice she praised his courage, his endurance. 'All this can be removed,' she said, indicating the lice, the peeling scabs, the dried excrement that encrusted his body. 'There is no dishonour in dirt. Giving up – that is the only dishonour.' The soldier was won over by the conviction in her words. He allowed himself to be washed, his wounds to be properly bandaged; at the end of the long process he felt strong enough to pull on for himself the clean shirt and breeches, washed and mended by Florence's team of soldiers' wives. As she moved on, he murmured thanks, and kissed her shadow as it passed. His gesture was copied the length of the ward.

Dr John Hall was disgusted. Shadow-kissing? What was going on? Soldiers were cannon-fodder; their lives didn't matter. They weren't supposed to have tender feelings. At the end of Florence's round, he accosted her on the landing.

'This won't do, Miss Nightingale. You're turning them soft. I have many years experience of the British private solder, and he's the lowest of the low – no better than an animal. Believe me, I know what I'm talking about.'

Florence gave not an inch. 'Dr Hall,' she replied, in a voice like an icicle, 'Treat men like animals, and they behave like animals. Treat them like the brave, decent Christians I believe them to be, and see the result for yourself.'

No one understood better than Florence the kind of prejudices the army had against women. She needed to prove them wrong. She had selected her nurses carefully; they were not a glamorous bunch. Young women and 'grand ladies' were not chosen. Their uniform was deliberately ugly – a grey dress and jacket, plain white cap, short woollen cloak. Round the shoulders was a 'frightful' brown scarf, with 'Scutari Hospital' embroidered in red. No coloured ribbons, jewellery or flowers were allowed. Florence wanted her nurses to be taken seriously. They were not there to flirt. Indeed, 'misconduct' with the troops meant instant dismissal. Once, a soldier grabbed a nurse in a Scutari street, but his mate recognised the uniform. 'Leave her alone,' he said, 'Don't you see she's one of Miss Nightingale's women?'

Florence slept in the storeroom on a bed behind a screen. She wore a black dress with white collar, cuffs, and cap, and a white apron. She was always cold, usually hungry and thirsty – the water allowance was only one pint a day, for drinking and washing –

but she never stopped working through that long, terrible winter.

Spring came at last. The hills round Scutari were bright with wild lilies and orchids. In May, Florence told Sidney Herbert that she had achieved 'the first really satisfactory reception of the sick'. She set up a reading-room and coffee house for the convalescent soldiers. The officers thought this was a waste of time – soldiers didn't want to do anything except get drunk – but Florence pointed out that there was nothing to do except get drunk. The reading-room proved very popular. Florence's rich friends sent out chess sets, books, puzzles, maps and pictures. Lessons were organised for those who could not read or write. There were singing classes, amateur dramatics and football matches.

Florence set up 'remitting offices' so that the men could send their pay home to their families. This had never been done before, so all the pay was spent on prostitutes and alcohol in brothels and inns. Lord Panmure, the new Secretary for War, growled that 'the British soldier is not a remitting animal'; the scheme would never work. But it did work. Seventy-one thousand pounds was sent home in six months –

about £3.5 million in today's money. And all of it, said Florence, saved from the drink shops.

Once things had improved at Scutari, Florence set off across the Black Sea to the two big hospitals at Balaclava. These were staffed by nurses not under her strict control; and they had begun to behave badly. Well-wishers, from Queen Victoria down to humble cottagers, had sent out presents for the men, and yet no one was in charge of distributing them. Some things were stolen, others given out unfairly. And there was one rebellious Welsh nurse, Elizabeth Davis, who enjoyed feeding her pet officers on port, sherry, brandy, jellies and sweetmeats intended for the wounded soldiers.

Florence took with her Alexis Soyer, his black secretary, her friend Charles Bracebridge, who with his wife Selina had come out to help Florence, and a drummer boy named Robert Robinson, who described himself as 'Miss Nightingale's man' although he was only twelve years old. He carried her messages and had charge of her precious lamp. Soyer described him as 'full of wit and glee'.

News of her arrival spread like wildfire. The soldiers rushed from their tents. At the Mortar

Battery, Soyer persuaded her to climb the rampart and sit on the centre mortar. 'Gentlemen, behold this amiable lady sitting fearlessly upon the terrible instrument of war! Behold the heroic daughter of England, the soldiers' friend!' The soldiers cheered her to the echo. They had picked bunches of flowers. Asked to choose which she liked best, she replied by gathering them all into her arms.

Immediately she set about reorganising the dirty and inefficient Balaclava hospitals, but after only a few days, disaster struck. Florence collapsed with 'Crimea fever'. This was probably typhus, possibly typhoid. Four soldiers carried her to the pure air of the Castle Hospital on the Crimean Heights. Soyer's secretary held an umbrella over her face, and little Robert Robinson walked behind, weeping because he was not strong enough to help carry or tall enough to hold the umbrella. When the men at Scutari heard the news, they turned their faces to the wall and cried.

For two weeks she hovered between life and death. In her delirium she would not stop writing, covering page after page with meaningless scribble. She thought she had an engine inside her head. All her hair was cut off. It grew back curlier but darker than before

– she lost the red-gold sheen of her youth for ever.

Once she was out of danger, Queen Victoria announced that she was 'truly thankful to learn that that excellent and valuable person Miss Nightingale is safe.' In England, strangers stopped each other in the streets to pass on the good news.

She was desperate to get back to Scutari. Dr Hadley, who had been attending her, put her on a ship, the *Jura* – but Dr Hadley was in league with her enemy, Dr John Hall, Chief of Medical Staff. They saw a chance to get this meddling woman out of their way, and they seized it. The *Jura* was not bound for Scutari but was going direct to England. Florence had been tricked by the men who wanted to get rid of her. In the nick of time her friend Mr Bracebridge discovered the truth. He summoned Lord Ward, who had a steam yacht; together they hurried the fainting Florence off the *Jura*, onto the yacht, and back to Scutari.

Still too weak to work, she convalesced in a house with a pleasant garden, and views on to the Bosphorus – the most splendid view in the world, said Florence, and at last she had time to admire it properly. Sidney Herbert sent her a terrier; the troops gave her an owl, to replace poor Athena. There was a baby, too – its mother was a soldier's wife, and while she worked in the washrooms it played by Florence's bedside, to her delight.

After two months she returned to the Barrack Hospital, but she kept on the house with the lovely views and sent the nurses in turns there to rest.

Meanwhile the war had passed its most ferocious phase. In September, Sebastopol fell to the British and French allies; victory was in sight. The inrush of sick and wounded soldiers had slowed; now Florence's main problem was controlling rivalries and rebellions amongst her staff. Not least of her worries was the extraordinary Miss Salisbury, a nurse who had been put in charge of the 'free gifts' store, but was found to have stuffed as many gifts as she could into and under her bed. Worse, she had written 'poison pen' letters home, telling lies about Florence. Florence needed help – someone to trust amidst all the back-stabbing. She sent for her Aunt Mai, who brought with her a storekeeper to manage the 'free gifts'. Aunt Mai burst into tears at the sight of her favourite niece – thin, pale, strangely childlike with her cropped hair. But she set to work, and she and Florence formed an unbeatable team. 'Nightingale Power', they called it.

Back at home, 'Nightingale fever' reached its height. Florence was the heroine of the poor – she had shown the world how to treat their soldier husbands and sons with dignity. A 'Nightingale Fund' was raised, to start a training school for nurses. £9,000 came from the troops. Prince Albert, like his wife Queen Victoria a great admirer, designed a brooch for Florence – a St George's Cross in red enamel topped with a diamond crown, encircled with the words 'Blessed are the merciful'.

Such adoration would have turned anyone's head – but not Florence's. She didn't want jewels, praise, or popularity. The war might be nearly over, but her life's work had hardly begun. For her ambitions went far beyond nursing now. She wanted to transform, not only the entire health system, but the British Army itself. She was the mother of 50,000 children. 'No one,' she wrote, 'can feel for the army as I do. People must have seen that long dreadful winter to know what it was. I can never forget.'

Peace with Russia was finally declared on 29th April 1856. The troops were ferried home. The British public was on the edge of its seat waiting for the return of its heroine. Florence's family and friends could hardly contain their impatience. But Florence was not ready to leave yet. First, she had to make sure that all her nurses were provided for. She asked the government to find employment for them; those who could not be placed were to be given a pension from her own money. One, Jane Evans, an old farm worker, had kept a pet buffalo calf; Florence made sure she could take it home. Florence was marvellous about detail.

On 16th July, the last patient left the Barrack Hospital. On 28th July, Florence packed her few personal belongings. She travelled with Aunt Mai as far as Paris, giving their names as 'Mrs and Miss Smith'. From Paris she travelled home alone. She was 'in sympathy with God, fulfilling the purpose [she] came into this world for' – but she could not know that the fulfilling of the purpose had only just begun.

Chapter Five

"I must try to remember that God is not my private secretary."

Florence returned from Scutari in a state of panic. She was convinced she had not long to live – she hadn't fully recovered from 'Crimea fever'; she often felt weak and faint. For nearly two years she had been surrounded by death; it was not surprising that she was obsessed by the prospect of her own. If she had known she had another fifty-four years to live, she might have calmed down a little.

Her family were dismayed. Florence had always been peculiar, now she was manic. She didn't want to see old friends, wouldn't listen to the praise that was heaped upon her. She didn't want to have any fun. It was just work, work, work. Wen heard her pacing her room late at night and worried that she was having nightmares; but no, she was planning how she could transform the British army so that the disasters of the Crimea could never happen again. 'Oh my poor men, I am a bad mother to come home and leave you in your Crimean graves – seventy-three per cent in eight regiments from disease alone – who thinks of that now?' she wrote in one of the many 'private notes' that littered her bedroom.

Victoria and Albert invited her to Balmoral. She was delighted – here was a chance to influence people who had real power! The royal couple were impressed. 'I wish we had her at the War Office,' said the Queen. But this was only a joke. A woman in government was unthinkable. Florence realised that to get things done she needed to make friends with the men who mattered – and she did. For the rest of her life she used men as her mouthpiece. For a Victorian woman, it was the quickest path to power.

Slowly, Florence became aware that she could use her reputation to influence politicians. She still disliked her fame, but she could see how much her sister revelled in it, so she allowed Parthe to become the unofficial secretary of her fan club. Letters arrived for Florence in 'hailstorms', along with gifts, songs, poems, and offers of marriage from total strangers. Parthe dealt with all of it. She and Fanny forgave Flo for breaking loose – in fact, they forgot that they had ever made any objections. Parthe, who had still not found a husband, found Florence's reflected glory to be the next best thing.

Meanwhile, Florence worked all the hours there were. She visited army barracks, lunatic asylums, prisons, orphanages... often she walked more than twenty miles a day. She wrote endless notes about how to improve these institutions. She was particularly shocked by the barracks, where 1,100 soldiers died each year from diseases caused by the dirty, cramped conditions and bad water. These deaths, Florence believed, could and should be prevented. 'You might as well take 1,100 men every year out upon Salisbury Plain and shoot them!' she exclaimed.

She gobbled up statistics and reports and turned them into pie charts and bar-graphs. She was the first person to present statistics in picture form. Florence loved statistics – 'more enlivening than a novel', she declared.

In less than six months she wrote an enormous

book – 1,000 pages of *Notes on Matters affecting the Health, Efficiency and Hospital Administration of the British Army*. Soon afterwards she produced another book of similar size – *Notes on Hospitals*. She was doing the work of ten people – and she was supposed to be dying!

She couldn't keep it up. The day before her thirty-seventh birthday, nine months after her return from Scutari, she suffered a complete collapse. She went to Malvern, where Victorian invalids went to drink the health-giving waters, and there she was carried about by old soldiers and treated as a goddess. The pattern of Florence's future life was set at this time. An extraordinary change came over her. The woman who had stayed on her feet for twenty-four hours on end was now often too weak to move. From now on she spent more time in bed than out of it. She never stopped working, but she no longer travelled about, inspecting things for herself. Sometimes she did not leave her room for months, even years, at a stretch.

Nobody knew quite what was wrong. In the 19th century, you didn't need to know; many diseases were still mysterious. Florence's doctors suggested 'neuras-thenia', which was thought to be 'the product of excessive stress upon the functions of the mind'. Neurasthenia has no precise meaning, and is not a term used by doctors nowadays.

It seems likely that what Florence had was a 'psychoneurosis'. She had attacks of giddiness, breathlessness, heart palpitations – all brought on by unwanted people or events. Her illness was very useful to her. It gave her a status like royalty. She could turn away people she didn't want to see. She could keep her tiresome family at bay. 'Poor Flo – she's most unwell – her heart is troubling her. She really is not strong enough to receive visitors. But she sends you her best love.'

She lived, to begin with, in a set of rooms in the Burlington Hotel in Mayfair, London, and later moved first to one house then another in nearby South Street, where she spent the last thirty-five years of her life. She hardly ever visited Lea Hurst or Embley, where family pressures still suffocated her. And her illness, because it was largely 'in the mind', allowed her to live to be ninety years old!

Because everyone, including Florence herself, believed that her life was hanging by a thread, they worked all the harder to get her projects done. Ill health never kept Florence from her work. She sat in bed, draped in lace shawls, at least one cat curled round her neck, a couple more nuzzling at her inkpot and leaving pawprints all over her papers. And she wrote and wrote and wrote. She concerned herself with every detail of every project. When St Thomas's Hospital – her favourite hospital, where her very own nurses' training school was run – moved to new buildings, Florence wrote a hundred letters on the subject of the new flooring alone. That was before she'd started on the washbasins, the beds, the curtains, the cooking arrangements...

She was tended by a team of devoted admirers – Aunt Mai, who abandoned her own family to look after Florence; the poet Arthur Hugh Clough, who ran errands for her; and the long-suffering Dr Sutherland, who sat downstairs and protected Florence from the streams of visitors. He helped on all her projects, researching, writing, answering letters. And he got few thanks for it. Miss Nightingale, the soldiers' angel of mercy, was something of a monster on her own territory. From those who worked for her she required no less than total commitment. Dr Sutherland had a wife and family of his own. He even dared go on holiday once. Florence was furious. A holiday? Didn't he know there was work to be done? He never repeated the mistake. And he didn't grumble, either. He thought Florence 'one of the most gifted creatures God ever made', and was honoured to be, as he put it, 'one of your wives'.

Anyone who was anyone came to call. The Queen of Holland, the Crown Princess of Prussia, the Duke of Cambridge... they all put up with the likelihood of being turned away. Often, Florence wouldn't see even her dearest friends. 'I cannot live to work unless I give up all that makes life pleasant,' she explained.

The one man she was always happy to see was Sidney Herbert, the politician who'd got her to Scutari in the first place. Everyone agreed he was a delight – intelligent, good-looking, with beautiful manners. To Florence, he was essential in her attempts to reform the army. She pushed him relentlessly. He worked as hard as he could, but it wasn't enough for her. Friends were alarmed Sidney wasn't well. He had liver problems. He was in a lot of pain. Surely he'd done enough? But no, Florence was ruthless. The work was unfinished. Sidney must try harder.

But he couldn't. He resigned from the government. Florence, in disappointed rage, wrote him a bitter letter. Was this the end of their great partnership? Sidney was a true gentleman. 'It takes two to make a quarrel,' he said, 'And I won't be one of them.'

And then, quite suddenly, he died. His deathbed words were, 'Poor Florence, poor Florence, our joint work unfinished.' Florence blamed God. Why could He not have spared him? She was overcome with grief, but it never occurred to her that she had pushed Sidney Herbert too hard. After his death, she would never hear a word of criticism of him. 'Sidney Herbert,' she said, 'must be remembered as the first War Minister who ever seriously set himself to the task of saving life.'

Meanwhile, a new player had entered the scene of the Nightingale family drama. Sir Harry Verney was a rich baronet who, though no longer young, was still reckoned to be one of the handsomest men in England. He was a widower with grown-up children and a beautiful house, Claydon in Buckinghamshire. He was a liberal MP who championed the rights of the poor, built model cottages, founded schools and hospitals. He fell in love with Florence and asked her to marry him.

But Florence had no intention of marrying anyone. She'd put all that behind her years ago. So Sir Harry turned his attentions to the next best thing – Parthenope. Poor Parthe! She was thrilled to be engaged at last, even if, yet again, she found herself in the shadow of her amazing sister.

Parthe was nearly forty. Fanny, who had given up hope of seeing either daughter married, was overwhelmed with excitement. She and Parthe spent long, happy days together 'fussing and shopping' in preparation for the wedding. And, at last, they left Florence alone.

***

For the next twenty years, Florence was the leading expert on army and medical reform. India – then part of the British Empire – was a notoriously unhealthy place. The British troops serving in India had a terrible time – sixty-nine out of every 1,000 died of disease, and only one in five of the solders' children survived infancy. The barracks were stiflingly hot, there was nothing to do, the drinking water 'visibly swarmed with animal life'.

Florence wrote a paper with the hard-hitting title, 'How People May Live and Not Die in India'. When it was read aloud at a social science congress in Edinburgh, the audience gave three cheers.

Florence never set foot in India, but she became an expert. When she moved house, her statistical reports on India filled two vans. She gave advice to the Viceroy – the Queen's deputy – and pushed for improvements in the lives of the poverty-stricken Indian people as well as the British soldiers.

Florence cared about all victims, male or female, children or adults, of whatever race or religion. She believed that if someone was suffering, they deserved to be looked after, and that was that.

The list of Florence's achievements is extraordinary. She helped set up district nursing. She helped reform workhouses – those grim institutions where the poor had to go when they were too old or weak to look after themselves. She gave medical advice to both sides in the Franco-Prussian War, and received the Prussian Cross of Merit and the French Bronze Cross. She campaigned to separate maternity hospitals from general hospitals, so that mothers and babies wouldn't catch diseases from other patients. She wrote a bestseller called *Notes on Nursing*, which included a chapter called 'Minding Baby' in which she recalled the fun she'd had with the soldier's baby in Scutari all those years ago.

And if this wasn't enough, she wrote enormous – and almost unreadable – books about God and spirituality. Florence was a mystic. One person who understood her ideas was Dr Benjamin Jowett, Master of Balliol College, Oxford. 'My darling Jowett', she called him. He wanted to marry her. Yet again she refused, but they remained great friends, and gave each other a lot of happiness.

Florence needed happiness. Memories of the Crimea still haunted her. Hard as she worked, it could never be enough. She expected as much from other people as from herself, but other people couldn't cope. When Aunt Mai, after years of helping Florence, returned to her own family, Florence felt betrayed. She was completely closed to reason. She needed Aunt Mai, and Aunt Mai had abandoned her. They did not speak again for twenty years.

And yet this invalid slave driver was also the gentle

and sympathetic nurse who entered into the suffering of her patients. She had single-handedly transformed the image of the nurse – indeed, she had stamped nurses with her own image. The training of nurses became one of her passions. Never again must nurses be seen as dirty, drunken slatterns. So at the Nightingale Training School, the rules were strict. As well as learning how to treat illnesses, the young women had to make sure that their own behaviour was beyond reproach.

Florence knew all the trainees personally. She interviewed them all, from her bed or her sofa, and wrote to them all. Only girls with the right attitude would do. She was like a stern but kindly aunt. She sent in fruit, game, cream, fresh eggs and butter. When a nurse started her first job, Florence sent flowers to welcome her. Nurses on journeys were provided with sumptuous picnic baskets. Sick or exhausted nurses were sent to the seaside at Miss Nightingale's expense, or sometimes to Lea Hurst or Claydon. She invited them to tea; the poorer the girl seemed to be, the larger and richer would be the cakes. Knowing this, some girls called on her deliberately wearing their shabbiest cloaks...

Florence took great pleasure in the company of young women, enjoying their energy and enthusiasm for life. She had two especial favourites, Miss Pringle, nicknamed 'The Pearl', and Miss Williams, known as 'Goddess Baby'. She showered them with affection. 'Dishes for Miss Williams,' says a note to her cook, 'Rissoles, or fillets of sole *à la Maître d'Hôtel*, or oyster patties, or *omelette aux fines herbes*, or chicken *à la mayonnaise* with aspic jelly, or cutlets *à la Béchamelle*.'

And so the busy, restless years rolled on. Family problems began to interfere again. Parthe became crippled with arthritis. As of old, she demanded Flo's attention – but this time, Flo was happy to give it. Parthe was really suffering. That made her a victim, and Florence had endless sympathy for genuine victims. This was nothing like Parthe's hysterical outbursts in days of old.

The same went for Fanny. Fanny was growing 'childish'; she couldn't manage Embley and Lea Hurst any more. In 1872 Mrs Watson died. The faithful housekeeper had kept everything under control. Fanny couldn't be left alone with Wen; they were both as bad as each other.

Florence brought Fanny back to London where she could keep an eye on her. Indeed, the needs of her family forced Florence out of her bedroom. For the first time in years, she played an active part in their lives. She thought she had escaped, to be free to work; and to be tied down by family troubles again was almost more than she could bear.

'Am I she who once stood on that Crimean height?' she asked herself. 'The lady with a lamp shall stand! The lamp shows me only my utter shipwreck.'

While Florence cared for Fanny in London, Parthe and Harry Verney stayed at Embley with Wen. But one morning the old man slipped on the stairs and died. Florence missed him dreadfully – in his old age, she had grown closer to him again, and she had always been his favourite child. And now she had the two estates to manage, plus responsibility for the ever-more confused Fanny.

Fanny was very old and almost blind. She feared new places and unfamiliar voices – Florence could not leave her to be looked after by strangers. 'Where is Flo?' Fanny asked, though Flo was right beside her. 'Is she still in her hospital? I suppose she will never marry now.'

At last, Fanny died. She was ninety-two. In her last hours, she regained some consciousness, and asked to hear her favourite hymns.

Florence was sixty years old, and she was FREE!

Chapter Six

"Too kind... too kind!"

Old age changed Florence Nightingale. She became softer, gentler. She still worked hard, but she no longer pushed herself quite so relentlessly. She made more time for other people, more time for laughter and fun. Talking to her could still leave you feeling 'like a sucked orange', as one visitor put it, but a kind of peacefulness had come over her.

'Life is more precious to me in my old age,' she said. She patched up the quarrels of the past. She made peace with Aunt Mai, and became close to Parthe again, for the first time since childhood. She often visited Parthe and Sir Harry at beautiful Claydon House. It was a second home to her, and, true to form, she was interested in the life of the village and made plans for improving the drains.

There was a striking change in her appearance, too. The slender, graceful girl, who in middle age had become thin and angular, with lines of suffering deeply marked on her face, was now transformed into a plump, almost cuddly, old lady, with smooth white hair and a twinkly smile. And her health improved, too. She still spent a lot of time in bed, and ate all her meals alone, but she was no longer a total invalid. She enjoyed paying visits and walking in gardens, which she had not done for twenty years.

Visitors to her house were struck by the tidiness. The rooms were flooded with light and of course spotlessly clean. Many Victorian houses were dark and cluttered, with thick heavy curtains and covers to protect the furniture, but not 35 South Street. Florence preferred blinds to curtains. The walls were painted white. French windows opened on to balconies, and there were flowers, flowers everywhere. Some of Florence's admirers sent her fresh flowers every week for the whole of her life. On every chair or sofa was curled one of her beloved cats.

Florence received visitors after luncheon. She lay on a couch wearing a black silk dress and a delicate white lace scarf made up especially for her by Sir Harry Verney. 'No lady ever wears anything but real lace,' she said. She interested herself in every detail of people's lives. She wrote birthday letters, advised young people about their love affairs or exam papers; she sent concert tickets to a cousin who was working too hard, a picnic and special cushion to another who was travelling by night train. Her servants, her butcher, the policeman on duty outside – she involved herself with all of them.

In return, she was well looked after. There were five maids as well as her own personal maid, a cook and an old soldier known as 'Miss Nightingale's messenger'. She ran a tight ship. She ordered all the food herself and was scrupulous about the quality. She wrote notes to Mrs Nield, the cook, after every meal. 'Why was the glue-pot used?' she wrote against 'veal cutlets'. She criticised Mrs Nield, but then reproached herself for her impatience. 'Let me remember that as Mrs Nield to me, so I to God.'

She was still concerned with bigger issues, too, though as she grew older, 'Nightingale Power' was less effective. The government no longer automatically consulted her about the army, hospitals, or India.

When she called public attention to the great Indian famine of 1878, her plea was dismissed as 'a shriek'.

In 1885, her friend General Gordon was murdered defending Khartoum; there was a huge outburst of indignation against the British government for not sending help quickly enough to save him. Florence shared concern about the government's failure, but was able to take consolation from the belief that General Gordon, a deeply religious man, had, through courage and suffering, succeeded in the sight of God even though his mission had failed.

'With him, all is well,' she wrote. In his memory, she helped set up the 'Gordon Home for Destitute Boys'. 'Ask them to tea, the roughest boys first'.

But though 'Nightingale Power' was waning, the effects of her life's work were felt all over the world. In 1884, when the – belated – Gordon Relief Expedition went to Egypt, a troop of nurses, led by Miss 'Goddess-Baby' Williams, was sent by the government. It was now assumed by everyone that female nurses were a Good Thing. Wounded soldiers everywhere received proper medical care – this was now taken for granted.

In 1887, Queen Victoria celebrated her Golden

Jubilee – fifty years on the throne. It was also Florence's private jubilee – fifty years since the 'voice' had called her to God's service. Of course Florence was not satisfied with her achievements: 'I, who was called at sixteen, I am now a whited sepulchre full of dead men's bones.' But the difference she had made to the lives of ordinary people was enormous. It is hard to think of anyone who had more impact. Most hospitals and training schools were now staffed by 'Nightingale nurses' who insisted on hygiene, order, and immaculate behaviour. We expect, now, to be well looked after in hospital. When mistakes are made, we are shocked – because we have high standards. Those standards were set for us by Florence Nightingale.

If you are a girl, and you have decided on a career that is interesting and worthwhile, then you have Florence to thank. Before she broke the mould, 'nice' girls didn't work. They stayed at home waiting for a suitable husband to come along. Once married, they had no independent life, or money of their own. For a woman to be a doctor, a politician, a lawyer, a professor... this was about as likely as flying to the moon. Poor women worked long, hard hours in factories, or sewed clothes by candlelight for rich folk to wear, or washed other people's dirty laundry. Such women worked for a pittance and looked after their families. But before Florence showed the way, there was only a handful of women in the whole country who had jobs that fulfilled them and contributed something to society.

Poor Parthe, wracked with pain, died on Florence's seventieth birthday. Florence devoted herself to Sir Harry Verney. He became her pet, her project, her dearest friend. Sir Harry, fit and handsome into his nineties, led an active life and helped to keep Florence going. After his death, her health broke down. She took to her bedroom at South Street in 1896 and never left it again. She still had fourteen years to live.

In 1897, an exhibition called 'The Victorian Era', organised for Queen Victoria's Diamond Jubilee, added hugely to the Nightingale legend. Florence disliked the fuss, but she did lend a marble bust of herself. This was one of the few likenesses ever made of her, since she hated to be photographed and wouldn't sit for portraits. She also lent the carriage she'd used in the Crimea, which was 'discovered all to pieces in an Embley farmhouse'. Everyday, flowers were laid by the bust; old soldiers were seen kissing the carriage.

This wasn't Florence's style at all. She never wanted to be a saint. 'I utter a pious wish,' she wrote to a cousin, 'that the bust may be smashed.' But even Nightingale Power couldn't destroy the power of fame. She was, and has remained, one of the most famous people of the Victorian age.

And then, like her mother Fanny's before her, her eyesight began to fail. By February 1889 she was 'too blind to read newspapers', though only the year before she had reread the whole of Shakespeare. Her bold, clear handwriting degenerated into a spidery scrawl, but her output of letters was still amazing. She wrote to Sir Harry's granddaughter begging her to christen her baby girl Balaclava – 'one of the most beautiful names in the world'.

She fought to keep her grip on life, but, as blindness settled in, so too did her memory fade. She would recite poetry, sing the songs she had loved in her youth, have the *Times* read to her everyday – she wasn't ready to go just yet. But for the last four years of her life, she shut down. Confused, blind, almost unconscious, she lay still for hours, recognising nobody.

In 1907, King Edward VII bestowed on her the

Order of Merit – the first time the great honour had been awarded to a woman. The king's representative brought it to her bedside. No one was sure how much she understood, but she knew something was going on. 'Too kind, too kind,' she murmured, raising her frail hand in acknowledgement.

After February 1910, she no longer spoke. The heroine of the Crimea, the woman who had laboured on through cruel extremes of cold and sickness and hardship, was now more helpless than a newborn baby. On 13th August 1910, aged ninety, she died in her sleep.

She left an enormous will – one of the longest ever. With her old attention to detail, she had left her books, pictures and furniture to hundreds of friends and relations. She wanted her body to be dissected in a medical school; she wanted no grand funeral, no memorial.

Her body was not left to science. But out of respect for her wishes, the offer of a state funeral in Westminster Abbey was refused. Her coffin was carried to her family grave by six sergeants of the British Army. The inscription on the tomb-stone was as simple as she would have wanted it:

F. N. Born 1820. Died 1910.

Before the darkness closed in on her, a friend had described death as 'a rest'. Miss Nightingale sat bolt upright against her pillows. 'A rest? Oh no,' she said, 'I am sure death is an immense activity.'

TIMELINE

1820 (12th May) - Florence is born.

1837 (7th February) - Florence receives her 'call' from God.

1849 - Florence refuses to marry Richard Monckton Milnes.

1851 - Florence goes to Kaiserworth Hospital.

1853 - Florence starts work at the Institute for Care of Sick Gentlewomen in Distressed Circumstances, Harley Street, London.

1854 (March) - Beginning of Crimean War.

1854 (August) - Cholera epidemic in London.

1854 (15th October) - Sidney Herbert asks Florence to lead nurses to Crimea.

1854 (21st October) - Florence and three nurses leave England.

1854 (5th November) - Florence and the nurses arrive at the Barrack Hospital, Scutari.

1855 (May) - Florence arrives at Balaclava. Soon becomes very ill.

1856 (29th April) - Crimean War ends.

1856 (28th July)- Florence leaves Scutari for England.

1857 (11th May) - Florence's health collapses.

1859 - *Notes on Hospitals* and *Notes on Nursing* are published.

1859 - Parther marries Sir Henry Verney.

1860 (24th June) - Nightingale Training School for nurses opens.

1861 - Sidney Smith dies.

1874 (10th January) - Wen dies.

1874 - District Nursing extablished.

1878 - Famine in India.

1880 (2nd February) - Fanny dies.

1885 - General Gordon murdered at Khartoum.

1890 (12th May) - Parthe dies.

1896 - Florence leaves her bedroom for the last time.

1897 - "The Victorian Era" exhibition.

1907 - Florence awarded Order of Merit.

1910 (13th August) - Florence dies.

Charlotte Moore's latest book, *George and Sam* (Penguin), tells of life with her two autistic sons.
She is also the author of several novels.
She lives in East Sussex.
This is her first book for children.
(Florence Nightingale is her first cousin four times removed.)

Dear Reader,

No matter how old you are, good books always leave you wanting to know more. If you have any questions you would like to ask the author, **Charlotte Moore,** about **Florence Nightingale** please write to us at: SHORT BOOKS, 15 Highbury Terrace, London N5 1UP.

If you enjoyed this title, then you would probably enjoy others in the series. Why not click on our website for more information and see what the teachers are being told? **www.theshortbookco.com**

All the books in the WHO WAS... series are available from TBS, Distribution Centre, Colchester Road, Frating Green, Colchester, Essex CO7 7DW (Tel: 01206 255800), at £4.99 + P&P.

OTHER TITLES IN THE WHO WAS...SERIES

WHO WAS... Admiral Nelson
The Sailor Who Dared All to Win
Sam Llewellyn
1-904095-65-8

No one ever imagined that a weak skinny boy like Horatio Nelson would be able to survive the hardships of life at sea. But he did. In fact he grew up to become a great naval hero, the man who saved Britain from invasion by the dreaded Napoleon.

Nelson was someone who always did things his own way. He lost an eye and an arm in battle, but never let that hold him back. He was brilliant on ships, clumsy on land, ferocious in battle, knew fear but overcame it, and never, never took no for an answer.

This is his story.

**WHO WAS... David Livingstone
The Legendary Explorer
Amanda Mitchison
1-904095-84-4**

Born a poor Glasgow cotton-mill worker, David grew
up to become a great explorer and hero of his time.

This is his incredible story. The tough man of Victorian
Britain would stop at nothing in his determination to
be the first white man to explore Afirca, even if it
meant dragging his wife and children along with him.

He trekked hundreds of miles through dangerous
territory, braving terrible illness and pain, and was
attacked by cannibals, rampaging lions and killer
ants...

WHO WAS... Anne Boleyn
The Queen Who Lost her Head
Laura Beatty
1-904095-78-X

For Anne Boleyn, King Henry VIII threw away his wife, outraged his people, chucked his religion, and drove his best friend to death.

What does it take to drive a King this crazy? Was she a witch? An enchantress? Whatever she was, Anne turned Tudor England upside-down and shook it. And everyone was talking about her...

But Anne lived dangerously. And when she could not give the King the one thing he wanted – a son – his love went out like a light. The consequences for Anne were deadly...

WHO WAS... Ada Lovelace
Computer Wizard of Victorian England
Lucy Lethbridge
1-904095-76-3

Daughter of the famous poet Lord Byron, Ada
Lovelace was a child prodigy. Brilliant at maths, she
read numbers like most people read words.

In 1834 she came to the attention of Charles Babbage,
a scientist and technowhizz who had just built an
amazing new 'THINKING MACHINE'. Ada and Mr
Babbage made a perfect partnership, which produced
the most important invention of the modern world –
THE COMPUTER!

WINNER OF THE BLUE PETER
BOOK AWARD 2002!